BOURNE AT DENBY

*Retrospections of an Exhibition
held at Derby Museum & Art Gallery,
22 March–25 May 1997*

Graham and Alva Key

EMS AND ENS LTD

First published February 1998

© Text and photographs:
Graham and Alva Key 1998

ISBN 1-874558-04-3

The rights of Graham and Alva Key to be identified
as the authors of this work has been asserted in accordance
with the Copyright, Design and Patents Act 1988
Sections 77 and 78

All rights reserved. No part of this publication may
be reproduced, stored in a retrieval system, or transmitted
in any form or by any means, electronic, mechanical,
photocopying, recording, or otherwise without the
prior permission of the publisher in writing.

Published by
Ems and Ens Ltd, Stapleton House, Langtree,
Torrington, Devon EX38 8NP

Printed in Great Britain by
Selsey Press Ltd, Chichester,
West Sussex PO20 0QH

Acknowledgements

WE would like to offer our special thanks to: Derby Museums & Art Gallery for staging the Denby Stonewares Exhibition, and to their principal curator, Anneke Bambery, for her hard work and encouragement with the organisation of the Exhibition; The Denby Pottery Company Limited, and in particular to their museum curator, Linda Salt, for providing valuable archive material as well as the facility of photographing on their premises and the loan of exhibits.

We would like to thank all of the many Denby collectors without whose unselfish generosity the Denby Stonewares Exhibition and ultimately the publication of this book would not have been possible: V Alldread, Caroline and Ed Claydon, Peggy Dawson, Mrs G Fake, Eileen Flint, Maggie France and Phil Yates, David Francis, Paul Green, Richard Halliwell, Ray and Ann Horsley, Hazel Ingram, Bill Jones, Derek Lakin, Laraine Manley, David and Ann Matthews, Dorothy Parkin, the relations of the late Mr W E Powditch, Jane Rodgers, Jill Sellars, Peter Sharp, David Spencer, Anne Swan, B Ward, Roy and Margaret Warner, Pat Wass, Mrs D Wathall, Maureen Watson, Joan and Jef Whitham, Mrs K Williamson, David and Glenda Wilmot, Shirley Vallance, and Norman Vertigan.

We are indebted to Trevor Hillman for his photographic work and we would also like to acknowledge the help of Alan Blakeman (of BBR, Elsecar), Paul Robinson (of Zeitgeist Antiques, London), Nicola Sidebotham, and Jerry Woodward.

Foreword

IT is only fitting that the results of the tireless efforts by Graham and Alva Key (leading authorities on early Denby stonewares), in staging the major exhibition of Denby Pottery held at the Derby Museum & Art Gallery in the spring of 1997, should be preserved for posterity in this fascinating record.

Many of the pieces gathered for the exhibition were from private collections; the rarer examples may never be seen in public again. The exhibition provided a deeper appreciation of Denby Pottery's myriad of products over the years – from bespoke salt-glazed items and the prolific ink bottles to detailed artware pieces.

In a fiercely competitive industry, Denby Pottery's blueprint for survival has always been to continually reassess its product range to meet the demands of changing lifestyles, and this frequently stretched the skills of the potter to the limit.

Graham and Alva continue to investigate and record the rare and the curious pieces of Denby, and to delve even deeper into the history surrounding their creation, all of which tell a story and play an important part in the Denby Pottery's rich heritage.

Linda Salt
Museum Curator
The Denby Pottery Company Limited

Contents

		Page
	Introduction	6
1	Nineteenth-Century Wares	7
	Salt-Glaze; Bottles; Commemorative and Personalised Wares; Denby Majolica	
2	Early Twentieth-Century Decorative Wares	20
	Arts and Crafts; Domestic and Functional Pottery; Tube-Lined Wares	
3	Decorative Art Pottery of the 1930s	32
	Animals and Novelties	
4	Towards World War II and Beyond	43
	Appendix: Actual Base Sizes of Denby Rabbits	48

Colour Illustrations

Plate		Page
1	Majolica jardinière and stand	9
2	Majolica porcupine	10
3	Cache pot and vase	10
4	Set of Housekeeper's jars	15
5	Two bowls from 'The Poet Series'	15
6	Tube-lined wares: Celtic vase and Dovedale bowl	16
7	Tube-lined wares: Avon bowl	16
8	Chinese Pedestal and Plant Pot	21
9	Toby jug with tube-lined decoration	22
10	Peveril vase and Goblet candlestick	22
11	Umbrella/walking stick stand	22
12	Owl vase by Donald Gilbert	27
13	Oval lidded pot by Donald Gilbert	27
14	Pigeon by Donald Gilbert	27
15	Cleopatra bowl by Donald Gilbert	27
16	Boxed set of split-eared rabbits	27
17	A selection of rabbits	28
18	Garden Pottery: Dolphin bowl on Pedestal by Donald Gilbert	28
19	Garden Pottery: Penguin by Donald Gilbert	33
20	Animal novelty: Sea lion by Donald Gilbert	34
21	Boatman ashtray	39
22	Large vase by Alice Teichner	39
23	Fruit bowl in Tibet glaze	40
24	Jug by Glyn Colledge	40

Introduction

SINCE the publication of our book *Denby Stonewares: A Collector's Guide* in October 1995, the interest in all aspects of collectable Denby has continued to grow steadily and there has been an upsurge in the number of enthusiastic collectors.

We were delighted when the Derby Museum & Art Gallery agreed to host the first-ever major exhibition of Denby Stonewares; this popular exhibition was staged from 22 March to 25 May 1997. During this period it was estimated that some 10,000 people visited the Museum, and both serious collectors and casual browsers alike were amazed by the superb quality and diversity of the artefacts on display.

Through the exhibition we have been fortunate to meet the descendants of old workers who have some wonderful reminiscences and stories of life at Denby Pottery in past decades; we have also been privileged to enjoy and photograph many beautiful and rare pieces in their private collections.

This book lists many of the exhibits in the Denby Stonewares Exhibition and is a photographic celebration of this important event. We have also set out to feature some of the superlative pieces, together with the fascinating new archive information and pottery marks which have come to the forefront during the last two years.

We trust that this supplementary volume will prove as interesting and useful a guide to collecting and identifying Denby pieces as did *Denby Stonewares*.

Graham and Alva Key
February 1998

1
Nineteenth-Century Wares

Salt-Glaze

The quest for finding salt-glazed and sprigged artefacts produced by Joseph Bourne at Denby during the 19th and early 20th centuries is full of intrigue, and the task of identification becomes more complex and indecisive as the years proceed.

Figure 1

Relief-moulded sprigs, previously attributed to the Brampton, Chesterfield, potteries may well have been used on some of the salt-glazed wares made at Denby as well. Apart from the oak tree and willow tree sprigs used during the 19th century, there are at least two additional different tree sprigs used at the factory, the first of which is shown in Figure 1.

The tree sprig next to the windmill in Figure 1 is almost certainly a representation of the thorn tree which stood for many years in the local market place at Ripley in Derbyshire. The tree has long since disappeared but is remembered in the Thorn Tree Inn which stands near to the place where the tree grew; dog racing was held regularly at this high, open spot in Ripley.

The salt-glazed tyg (Figure 2) on which the tree sprig is to be found has an important piece of local Derbyshire history attached to it. It is known that, in 1857, J T Capon Esq. was Mayor of Ripley, Derbyshire, which is two miles away from Denby Pottery. He worked at the local gasworks and owned three dogs whose names – Catchem, Topper and Gas – are underglazed on the collars of the three greyhound handles on the tyg.

The fact that this salt-glazed tyg has a known provenance

Figure 2

Figure 3   *Figure 4*

gives positive evidence that the tree sprig next to the toper (Figure 3) is also one used by Joseph Bourne and Son and has been seen on other undocumented pottery of this era. The George and Dragon sprig (Figure 4) is also to be found on other tygs, loving cups and jugs produced at Denby Pottery in the second half of the 19th century.

Exciting salt-glazed finds which were included in the Derby Exhibition are shown in Figures 5–11. None of the pieces shown bears any impressed marks, but the pieces can be identified from the clay and the glaze colour, the sprigging, and evidence from late 19th-century catalogues.

Figure 5

The pistol flask shown in Figure 5 is a beautifully modelled spirit flask which is approximately 22.5 cm (9 in.) long and was made at Denby Pottery circa 1830.

The money box with attached bird whistle (Figure 6) was made in 1824 and is inscribed 'Joseph Walker/ Henmore/April 14th 1824'; it was probably manufactured at the Belper pottery (which was owned by Joseph Bourne at this time).

Figure 7 shows a shaving mug which was made circa 1840, and is 15 cm (6 in.) high, having the usual tree/ windmill/toper sprigs with the grape vine around the base, a feature which is very typical of many of the Denby salt-glazed and Denby Colours pieces.

The tobacco jar in Denby Colours shown in Figure 8 bears the inscription 'W. S. Lythgoe Manchester

Figure 6

PLATE 1. *Majolica jardinière and stand*

PLATE 2. *Majolica porcupine with 'Elliott London' impressed name and fleur-de-lys*

PLATE 3. *Cache pot, with sgraffito decoration and inscription (left), and vase, also with sgraffito decoration (right)*

Figure 7

October 23 1866'. The jar also bears an unusual sprig of a greyhound and the lid is in the form of a candlestick.

Figure 9 shows a puzzle jug dating from the mid-19th century and having a rarely seen sprig of a gypsy encampment.

A lidded pot, circa 1840 (having sprigs of an 'earlier' windmill, an unusual tree, a man sitting on a barrel smoking a pipe, and a man sitting on a barrel drinking), and a mask jug with greyhound handle and pewter lid (having sprigs of drinking and smoking monkeys in medieval costume), are shown in Figure 10.

Figure 11 shows a ship jug (circa 1870), so-called because it has a wide base which gives it stability.

Figure 8

Figure 10

Figure 9

Figure 11

Bottles

Joseph Bourne acquired a reputation for quality stoneware bottles early in the 19th century. The earliest known bottle produced at the pottery, which is shown in Figure 12, bears the name George Calton and is dated 1813; this example can be seen in the museum at Denby Pottery.

Although many of the smaller salt-glazed bottles and jars bear no pottery mark, a large proportion of the porters, ginger beers, ink bottles, and the like, carry very distinctive markings (see *Denby Stonewares,* pp. 29 and 167–9). The common oval Bourne Denby impressed mark has been the subject of further research; certainly the marks having a number within the oval give a positive indication of the year of manufacture, but the ones having

Figure 12

an impressed letter within the oval have been the subject of much deliberation; one suggestion is that these may well have been used during the 1890s. Although bottles with impressed letters are not common, the letters A to E are the ones most frequently seen; even the letters J and M have been seen on rarer examples. This would therefore suggest that there must have been some overlap between the different types of marks.

The bottle featured in Figure 13 seems to be quite unique and remains something of a puzzle as it is the first one seen with an impressed letter *and* a number within the oval.

Figure 13

It is rare to find any blacking bottles with any impressed marks; the earliest known examples date from between 1817 and 1834 and have the words 'BLACKING BOTTLE' impressed in a semi-circular shape with the initials 'J.B.D.' (Joseph Bourne, Denby), with a small impressed number in the centre (Figure 14).

Stoneware Hamilton bottles are quite a rarity; these are ovate in shape and were produced from 1817–34. The one illustrated in Figure 15 has a semi-circular impressed mark which reads

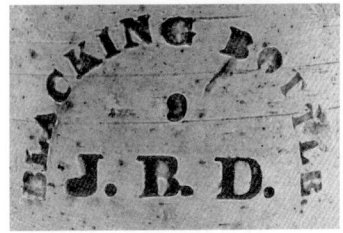

Figure 14

'BELPER & DENBY POTTERIES, DERBYSHIRE VITREOUS STONE BOTTLES &c/J.BOURNE PATENTEE/ Warranted not to Absorb/EX'. Impressed on the reverse side is 'BATHGATE & CO CALCUTTA', which suggests that

Figure 15

these were mainly exported to India during the days of the British Raj and that the bottles most probably contained quinine.

Another rare type of bottle produced around the turn of the century by Denby Pottery was a cross between a ginger beer bottle and an ink bottle, but unusually the bottle had a small handle attached as well as a pouring lip (Figure 16). The purpose of these bottles was for the retailing of rennet which was used in the dairy industry.

Commemorative and Personalised Wares

In *Denby Stonewares* (pp. 18 and 20) reference is made to a flattened ovoid commemorative flask which was reproduced for the American market by Denby Pottery in the 1960s. Figure 17 illustrates the original version of this flask, most probably manufactured circa 1840 to commemorate the marriage of Queen Victoria to Prince Albert. It features Victoria's head in relief within an oval plaque on the front, and the Duchess of Kent is displayed similarly on the reverse.

Figure 16

Figure 17

Personalisation of pottery is most useful in assisting the collector to date unmarked pottery, although the rare commemorative loving cup in Figure 18 is deceptive. It has a grey slip overall with applied relief-moulded decoration in cobalt blue; on one side is an underglazed laurel wreath surrounding a banner with the motto 'Imperium et Libertas' with a crown and the large letters 'P L' (for Primrose League), and on the reverse side is a coronet, a spray of primroses and the words 'Beaconsfield April 19 1881' all contained within a raised shield. The impressed mark on the base is the fleur-de-lys and the words 'Elliott London' (see *Denby Stonewares*, p. 168, mark J). This dates the piece around the turn of the century and was produced retrospectively of Disraeli's death. It is interesting to note that the mould for the Elliott loving cup (minus the sprigging) was re-used by the factory in 1933 for a commemorative piece for the Centenary of the Catholic Revival in the Anglican Community (Figure 19).

Figure 18

There can be little doubt that the Denby Colours inkwell with the acorn finial pictured in Figure 20 was produced in 1878 for a certain W Clarke.

A miniature loving cup, 4 cm (1.6 in.) high, commemorating Queen Victoria's Diamond Jubilee in 1897, is the smallest recorded Denby commemorative piece to date (Figure 21). The loving cup is in Denby Colours and, uncommonly, the name MORTLOCK'S appears underglazed on the main body of the pot, rather than on the base as is more usual.

Figure 19

Figure 20

The commemorative beaker produced for the 1902 Coronation of King Edward VII (Figure 22) is quite a rarity; the black underglazed transfer print is rarely seen on Denby commemoratives for this celebration. A trefoil-topped jug (Figure 23) was also produced for the 1902 Coronation (this style of jug with applied rose, thistle and shamrock was first made for Queen Victoria's Diamond Jubilee), on the front of which is an ornate decorated sprig in which are the heavily embellished letters 'E R (VII)' along with the

Figure 21

Figure 22

PLATE 4. *Set of 1930s Housekeeper's jars with raised tube-lined lettering*

PLATE 5. *Two bowls from 'The Poet Series': Snowdrop (left) and Daffodil (right)*

PLATE 6. *Tube-lined wares: Celtic vase in Electric Blue and Mottled Green glaze with Floral decoration (left); Dovedale bowl with Carnival decoration (right)*

PLATE 7. *Tube-lined wares: Avon bowl in Mottled Brown glaze with Heart decoration and Electric Blue glaze inside*

Figure 23

crown and 'CORONATION 1902'. To each side of this are the heads of the King and Queen in relief, and underglazed in black is a personalisation with the capital letters 'J.S.'.

An unusual commemorative loving cup in Denby Colours was produced in 1911 for the Coronation of King George V (Figure 24); the more common commemorative pieces made by Denby for this celebration were the handled mugs (see *Denby Stonewares*, p. 37, Plate 7).

Moving on to more recent times, as well as the rare Edward VIII barrel-shaped commemorative mug (*Denby Stonewares*, p. 39, Figure 36), the coronation plaque illustrated in Figure 25, which is in an Epic Green glaze bearing the date May 12th 1937, is also something of a rarity.

Figure 24

Figure 25

Commemorative pottery was not only confined to royal occasions; Figure 26 shows an example of a jug, dated 1909, the shape of which is illustrated in the Denby catalogues of the time and was retailed by Mortlock's Ltd of Oxford Street, London. There were certainly many of these made; 'BOURNE/DENBY' is impressed on the base, and on one side is a coat of arms while on the reverse side is a Welsh inscription under the transparent glaze, the translation of which reads as follows:

Land of the Welsh Giants
To commemorate the coming of age
of Wilfred Hugh Julian Gough
Caer-Rhun
Llechwedd y Garth
Faugh-A-Ballagh

['Caer-Rhun' is the name of the place; 'Llechwedd y Garth' is the name of the house; and 'Faugh-A-Ballagh' is Irish (the family had Irish connections as is illustrated on the coat of arms).]

Figure 26

Denby Majolica

The royal blue and tan shiny mottled glaze of this ware is very distinctive and the full extent of shapes which were retailed is only just being fully discovered. The largest piece to date is a magnificent jardinière and stand which has an overall height of almost 90 cm (36 in.) (Plate 1); this piece is now displayed in the Denby Pottery Museum. This shape of jardinière with the 'pie crust' top features on the front of J Bourne's catalogue for 1904 under the heading 'Danesby Flower Vases'. The jardinières and stands were listed in the catalogues as pedestals and plant pots. The elegant Majolica candlestick illustrated in Figure 27 is typical of the more imaginative design and the gradual emergence of the art pottery which was happening at Denby during the late Victorian and early Edwardian eras.

Figure 27

The most spectacular find to date is a large stoneware porcupine, 25 cm (10 in.) long (Plate 2), and what makes this item of particular importance is that it has the 'Elliott London' impressed name with the fleur-de-lys. Almost all the known Elliott pieces found to date have the grey overall slip with blue sgraffito designs and lettering, but several Majolica pieces designed by him have recently been discovered; the small footed trough with a decorative rim, 8 cm (3 in.) square by 7 cm (2.8 in.) high, shown in Figure 28, is one such item. Other miniatures made in the Majolica range included jugs, baskets, dishes and handled vases (Figure 29).

Figure 28

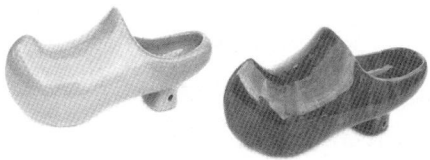

Figure 29

Novelty items were introduced in 1908; J Bourne & Son's advertisement in the *Pottery Gazette* proudly announces 'Special Lines for Spring Trade' and included amongst these are posy vases in the form of elegant Victorian/Edwardian lady's shoes and also a clog (which was designed to be hung up as a wall pocket) (Figure 30). These were not only available in the Majolica glaze but in a variety of other plain coloured glazes. It is also interesting to note that at this time the pig money boxes were being more widely promoted; these are

Figure 30

Figure 31

very popular with collectors, but a rare form of elephant money box was produced during this era (Figure 31). Also featured in the catalogue was a rather comical-looking frog whose open croaking mouth was intended to be used as a posy vase. On a more 'down to earth' note, the Majolica glaze was used on items which had a more functional use; the four diabolo-shaped items shown in Figure 32 are furniture rests.

Ironically, the other forms of Majolica in green and brown mottled glazes – which have, until recently, been considered to be rare – are now being 'discovered'. Relatively few of the pieces that have been found have shapes that have similar counterparts within the 'traditional' blue/tan Majolica ranges. From examination of the profiles, it is fairly clear that this ware was produced in the 1890s and the first few years of the 20th century. Collectors will be very intrigued to learn of the existence of an Elliott green Majolica art pottery vase which is described in greater detail in the next chapter. Figures 33 and 34 illustrate some of the finer artefacts which have been discovered in this rarer glaze. The largest and most impressive piece to date is the walking stick stand illustrated in Figure 35; it measures 61 cm (24 in.) in height.

Figure 32

Figure 33

Figure 34

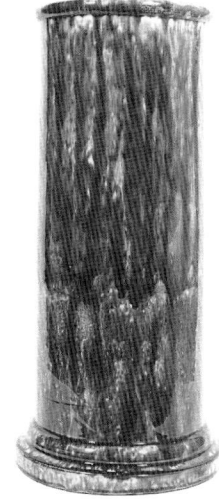

Figure 35

2
Early Twentieth-Century Decorative Wares

Arts and Crafts

The full extent of the influence of Horace Elliott upon pottery design in general is only gradually emerging. He is well-known for his work and design at the Ewenny Pottery in South Wales, but positive links with the C H Brannam Pottery in Barnstaple have been discovered as well as with other North Devon potteries, and possible connections with potteries in Yorkshire are currently being investigated.

Apart from the commemorative loving cup and the rare Majolica pieces described in the previous chapter, there are many interesting and varied artefacts which have now emerged. The 'Fin de Siècle' loving cup (*Denby Stonewares,* pp. 46 and 55) was certainly the *pièce de résistance* in the Arts and Crafts section at the Derby Exhibition, but other new Elliott finds include:

- Cache pot, with sgraffito decoration and bearing the inscription 'This pretty jar was made to hold/whate'er your please from pickles to gold' (Plate 3).
- Vase (Plate 3), with sgraffito decoration again, which illustrates well the Arts and Crafts Movement interest in hand-made products.
- Cream pot, with sgraffito decoration and bearing the inscription 'Mafeking Relieved God save the Queen and bless B.P.' [Baden Powell?], and on the reverse side 'This little pot was made a few hours after Colonel Mahon marched into Mafeking on Thursday morning May 17th 1900' (Figure 36).
- Pig money box with incised inscription 'Uriah John Abbott 1904', and on the reverse side the motto 'My diet I admit is strange, Silver will do if you have no change'.

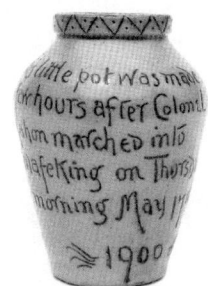

Figure 36

- Pig money box with broken ear (created at the time the piece was made) bearing the incised inscription 'This pig went to market', and also having the additional added inscription in underglazed black hand-writing 'This little boar was taken prisoner when Pretoria was captured June 8th 1900 with a wounded ear J. Green' (Figure 37).

The moulding for this particular pig money box is

Figure 37

PLATE 8. *Chinese Pedestal and Plant Pot in Royal Blue glaze with Belt decoration*

PLATE 9. *Toby jug with tube-lined decoration viewed from front (left) and side (right)*

PLATE 10. *Peveril vase in Electric Blue glaze, the size and height of which can be seen alongside a Goblet candlestick, also in Electric Blue glaze*

PLATE 11. *Umbrella/ walking stick stand in Electric Blue glaze*

quite different from the standard Denby/Elliott shape in that it is slightly smaller in size, has a more pronounced snout, and it sits with two back legs to one side.

- Small toby jug (no handle applied), 9 cm (3.6 in.) high, in which the figure represented is a town-crier with a bell in his left hand, with the incised inscription 'A Fine Old English Gentleman'; the toby jug is signed on the base 'Elliott London 1903' (Figure 38).

Figure 39

Figure 38

- Tall vase, 34.5 cm (13.8 in.) high, in green Majolica glaze having a rounded square base with a twisted square main stem (Figure 39). It bears the impressed 'Elliott London' mark together with the typical fleur-de-lys mark.
- Cream pot (Figure 40), with sgraffito motto which reads: 'Honor et Gloria/Long reign Victoria/We've taken Pretoria/God save the Queen/Whit Tuesday 1900'.
- Fern pot, with sgraffito cobalt blue decoration in the Arts and Crafts style (Figure 41).

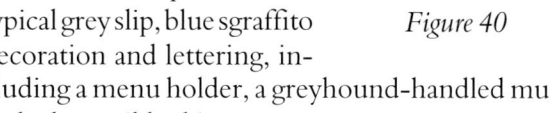

Figure 40

Figure 41

Private ceramic collections have also revealed some very desirable Elliott pieces in the typical grey slip, blue sgraffito decoration and lettering, including a menu holder, a greyhound-handled mug, and a large ribbed jug.

The work of J C A Wheeler continues to attract the attention of collectors. Unfortunately, pottery designed and produced by him is extremely rare, as his output was mainly limited to school holidays and was not really a large-scale commercial venture. Newly found pieces include:

- Small jug, 7.5 cm (3 in.) high, with sgraffito decoration (Figure 42).
- Small square tile on which is featured a pig (Figure 43); Wheeler's favourite subjects were ducks and geese.

- Small vase with underglazed cobalt blue duck and reed decoration (Figure 44).
- A square tile (Figure 45), which bears the JCW monogram and the name Denby underglazed on the front, and features daisy-type flowers.

Figure 46

Figure 42

- Pair of vases, approximately 20 cm (8 in.) high, with underglazed cobalt blue decoration of cockerels and hens (Figure 46).

Domestic and Functional Pottery

The various types of domestic pottery, for example, teapots, tobacco jars, jugs, and the like, were categorised in *Denby Stonewares*. Denby Pottery, as everyone is aware, is currently a producer of domestic and functional pottery, and has been – primarily – for nearly two centuries.

As it was therefore impossible to feature a comprehensive display of this category of wares in the Denby Stonewares Exhibition, it was decided to highlight just a few of the rare and unusual items of functional pottery produced during the first few decades of this century.

Figure 43

Figure 44

Figure 47

- Toast rack in emerald green (Figure 47); toast racks with five hoops were also produced.
- Salt-glazed bucket and a salt-glazed butter jar (minus lid) (Figure 48).

Figure 45

Figure 48

Figure 49

- Vase in royal blue with a cream, rough-textured band decorated with daisies (Figure 49). This vase is strikingly similar to those produced at the neighbouring Lovatts Pottery at Langley Mill; the date of the vase is circa 1912 and is marked 'BOURNE/DENBY'.
- Jug and bowl set (minus soap dish) in shiny black glaze with yellow inside (Figure 50).
- Souvenir ware jug in Denby Colours underglazed 'A PRESENT FROM YARMOUTH' (Figure 51).
- Queen Anne Teaset (Figure 52), which was a registered design and was made in the style of the earlier silver teasets.
- Small two-handled pot with underglazed blue decoration made for the Medici Society (Figure 53).
- Cemetery vase with a simulated granite glaze (Figure 54).
- Cemetery vase in a black glaze (Figure 55). This vase was described in the catalogues as 'The Manor Vase – for cemetery or garden use'.

Figure 50

Figure 51

Figure 52

Figure 53

Figure 54

Figure 55

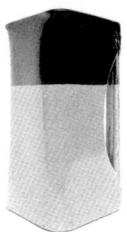

Figure 56

Figure 57

Figure 58

- Triangular-shaped jug in Denby Colours with registered patent (Figure 56).
- Chamber pot in Denby Colours (Figure 57).
- Bale tobacco jar (Figure 58) was one of a series of novelty tobacco jars, first produced in 1919, and made to look like a bale of cotton tied up with twine.
- Schweppes Green Ginger Wine flagon (Figure 59); these fine jars in a rich deep blue glaze with raised tube-lined lettering were also made by the Doulton factory.
- Salt-glazed coffee pot with internal filter (Figure 60).
- Housekeeper's jars (Plate 4) with raised tube-lined lettering.
- Dog bowl (Figure 61) in a pink glaze with raised tube-lined lettering.
- Green planter (Figure 62); this rather ornate and unusual shaped planter is in a green glaze.
- Two salt-glazed telegraph insulators (Figure 63).
- Wine jug with mottled brown glaze underglazed with the words 'Le Bon Vin' (Figure 64). This wine jug was made in 1940 by Denby Pottery for the Price, Powell Pottery in Bristol, after it had been destroyed by enemy bombs.

Figure 59

Figure 60

Figure 61

Figure 62

Figure 63

Figure 64

PLATE 12. *Owl vase, in Pastel Blue glaze, by Donald Gilbert*

PLATE 13. *Oval lidded pot, in Pastel Blue glaze, by Donald Gilbert*

PLATE 14. *Pigeon, in Pastel Blue glaze, by Donald Gilbert*

PLATE 15. *Cleopatra bowl, in Pastel Blue glaze, by Donald Gilbert*

PLATE 16. *Original boxed set of six split-eared rabbits*

PLATE 17. *A selection of rabbits, including one with real rabbit fur attached*

PLATE 18. *Garden Pottery: Dolphin bowl on Pedestal by Donald Gilbert*

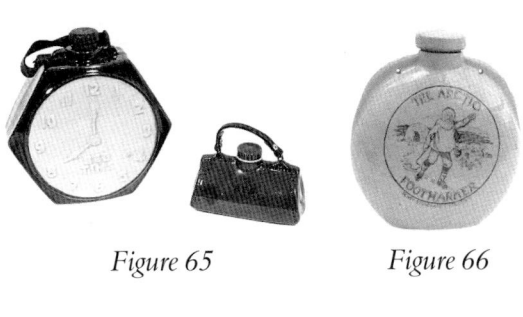

| Figure 65 | Figure 66 |

- Hot water bottles: Clock (Figure 65, left); miniature Gladstone Bag (Figure 65, right); Arctic (Figure 66); Dormice (designed by Donald Gilbert) (Figure 67); Boudoir (Figure 68).

Figure 68

Figure 67

Hot water bottle collecting is now extremely popular, particularly for the rarer novelty-type bottles. Denby Pottery was at the forefront of the production of these desirable items and some of them are now extremely rare.

Tube-Lined Wares

Research into the Danesby Ware base mark (which was originally used by the factory in 1886, but was extensively used during the 1920s and 1930s on the art pottery and decorative wares), has shown that there are several different

Figure 69

script versions in existence. This has been most useful in dating the tube-lined wares as well as earlier pieces of Orient Ware and Electric Blue.

There is no doubt that the hand which produced the underglazed and hand-signed mark (Figure 69) is that of Albert Colledge who produced the familiar stamped Danesby Ware script mark.

It is fascinating to trace the evolution of the Denby decorative wares through from Edwardian times to the late 1930s. Research has shown that the experiments with coloured glazes and more innovative shapes in vases and bowls before World War I, culminated in such a plethora of fine, superlative art wares in the period from 1924 to 1940. One such example is the Goblet candlestick (Figure 70), which first appeared around 1912; the one illustrated is in a matt green glaze

Figure 70

and has the unusual Rainbow Pottery Co. Lindfield (Sussex) mark on the base; several Denby pieces have been discovered with this mark and local historians in Sussex are currently researching this rather enigmatic pottery. By the 1920s the Goblet candlestick was embellished using the latest tube-lining techniques with art glazes (Figure 71). By the 1930s the Goblet candlestick (shown in Plate 10) was a standard production in the Electric Blue and Orient Ware ranges of decorative wares (see *Denby Stonewares*, p. 92, Plate 32).

Figure 71

'The Poet Series' of bulb bowls provide an excellent illustration of the progress made by Denby Pottery towards establishing themselves as a *tour de force* in art pottery production. They combined skilful tube-lining techniques, in which there was a raised flower design and the wording of the text applied in raised lettering, together with different coloured art glazes on both the interior and exterior. Prior to the publication of *Denby Stonewares*, not one of this unique series of three bowls had ever been out of private collections to be photographed, but it was a thrill to find two of these delightful artefacts for the Denby Stonewares Exhibition in 1997. The two bowls illustrated in Plate 5 are Daffodil, which bears the text by Wordsworth 'And then my heart with pleasure fills, And dances with the daffodils', and Snowdrop, which bears the text – also by Wordsworth – around the top 'Chaste snowdrop venturous harbinger of spring'.

Many collectors of tube-lined wares are surprised to find that Denby produced such fine Danesby Decorated Stoneware in the 1920s. Two spectacular exhibition pieces which were on display were:

- Celtic vase in Electric Blue and Mottled Green glaze with an elaborate version of Floral decoration (Plate 6, left);
- Dovedale bowl with Carnival decoration (Plate 6, right);

and later seen in a private collection:

- Avon bowl in Mottled Brown glaze with Heart decoration and with Electric Blue glaze inside (Plate 7).

The 1924 catalogue advertised Siamese, Japanese and Chinese Pedestals and Plant Pots with Gothic, Carnival and Belt decorations respectively (these are now commonly called jardinières and stands). Unfortunately, no catalogue illustrations for these magnificent items can be found. Apparently, very few of them were ever made and most were for export to America. Imagine our excitement when we learnt of the existence (in a private collection) of a Chinese Pedestal and Plant Pot in Royal Blue glaze with Belt decoration (Plate 8). One of only thirteen pieces made, twelve of which were exported to Boston in the USA, the piece was originally displayed in the window of a china shop belonging to Mr W E Powditch in Belper, Derbyshire, with the objective of attracting customers to the shop; the piece has since been bequeathed to his grand-daughter.

The extent of Denby's creativity continues to astound collectors; no existing catalogue information gives any indication that the pottery manufactured toby jugs. However, one such jug, 8 cm (3 in.) high, produced around 1930 (Plate 9), has been 'discovered' in a private collection. The tube-lined decoration is exquisite and is combined with a variety of coloured glazes. Another style of toby jug was produced under the Velray registered name, and this is described in the next chapter.

3
Decorative Art Pottery of the 1930s

SINCE the publication of *Denby Stonewares*, the hunt for the unusual pieces of pre-1940 Danesby Ware has been a priority for collectors; several superlative pieces have now appeared in private collections, as well as the many special pieces which have been found, some of which are described below.

Electric Blue glaze was introduced in the mid-1920s and decorated many innovative shapes. Over the next decade the range of shapes expanded and this vibrant glaze was also used on non-catalogued or 'one-off' pieces. Some of the earliest and most unusual objects seen to date in this glaze, which bear the hand-written Danesby Ware script mark on the base (Figure 72), are as follows:

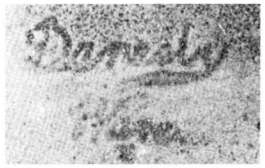

Figure 72

- Low, three-footed bowl (Figure 73).
- 'Aladdin' teapot (Figure 74), with the following inscription in gold lettering, added after the pot was glazed:
    To Sister Saville
    From Baby Eggleton
    Sep 15th 1928.
- Vase (Figure 75).
- Tankard (Figure 76); it is interesting to note that this was the shape adopted for the Manor Green and Quaker Brown mugs which were later mass-produced as tableware.
- Two-handled vase and goblet (Figure 77).

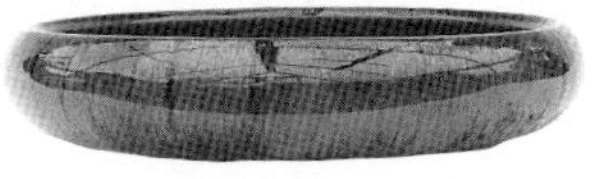

Figure 73

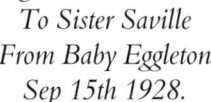

Figure 74

Figure 75

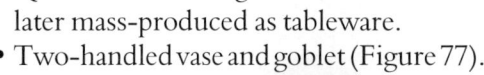

Figure 76

Figure 77

PLATE 19. *Garden Pottery: Penguin by Donald Gilbert*

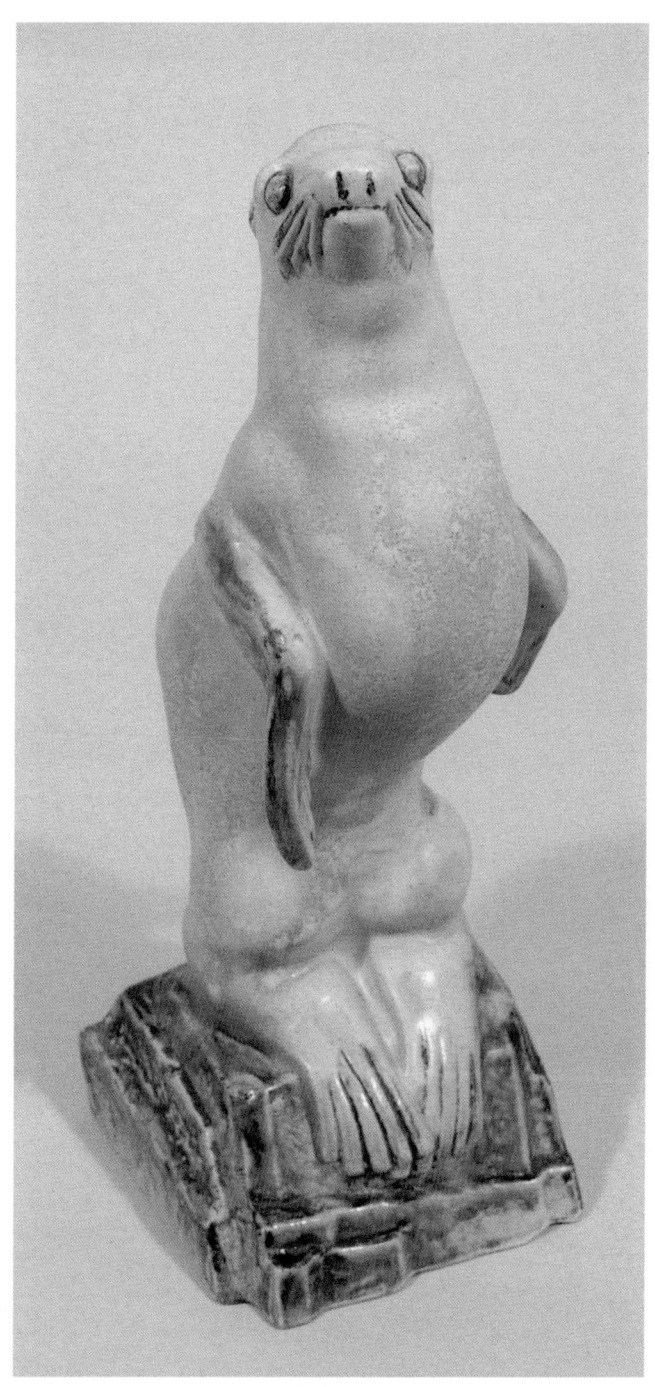

PLATE 20. *Animal novelty: Sea lion by Donald Gilbert*

The most spectacular piece so far recorded and shown in the Derby Exhibition was a Peveril vase (Plate 10), which measures 75 cm (30 in.) high; the largest production size for this type of vase was 45 cm (18 in.) high. One can only assume that vases of this size (which were hand-thrown) were produced as special orders. Another very special and rare item of Electric Blue is an umbrella/walking stick stand (Plate 11) which measures some 60 cm (24 in.) in height.

The Regent Pastel and Pastel Blue ranges of art pottery were inspired and designed by the young and talented sculptor Donald Gilbert. Gilbert's work is now admired by an ever-growing number of discerning collectors, and his remarkable skill in capturing the life-like features of both flora and fauna is a great achievement in decorative stoneware production. Gilbert's inspiration for his depiction of wild animals must surely have come from London Zoo, which was undergoing rapid expansion during the early 1930s and was one of the few places wild animals could be seen in captivity in Britain.

The surviving Denby catalogues of the early 1930s give so little evidence of the full range of innovative designs produced by Donald Gilbert. Since the publication of *Denby Stonewares* several previously unknown production items have been 'discovered', including:

- Owl vase (Plate 12), which has the distinctive Gilbert 'chevron' design around the main body of the pottery (this is also evident on his celebrated Epic Green cookware design!).
- Oval lidded pot in Pastel Blue glaze (Plate 13), approximately 17.5 cm (7 in.) long, the base having the typical sculptured 'chevron' design around its circumference, and the lid having a life-like three-dimensional lobster moulded on it.
- Cat and Mouse bookends and Kitten (Figure 78); the profile of these is identical to the children's hot water bottle produced in the early 1930s. The glaze used on the bookends in the illustration is Regent Pastel.
- Pigeon in Pastel Blue glaze (Plate 14).
- Penguin tobacco jar (Figure 79).
- Cleopatra bowl in Pastel Blue glaze (Plate 15).

Figure 78

Figure 79

Another interesting find which bears the Gilbert 'chevron' hallmark is the umbrella/walking stick stand in Pastel Blue glaze (Figure 80), which stands 55 cm (22 in.) high. It would seem that Maples (Furnishers) marketed the stick stands as their shop name appears on the base.

Animals and Novelties

It is this field of Denby collectables in which the greatest interest has been shown. Many of the novelty items illustrated in the catalogues of the 1930s are very scarce but have captured the imagination of an increasing number of collectors. As a result, there has been a dramatic increase in the values of animal and novelty pieces around the country.

Figure 80

Rabbits continue to be at the top of the collecting league and it is fascinating to see all the differing colour variations as well as functional variations too. Most collectors will be familiar with the 'Cottontail' which was produced for dispensing cotton wool; although being made by the Denby factory, they were not marketed by them. An interesting variation on this theme was displayed at the Denby Stonewares Exhibition: a size 2A rabbit in shiny green glaze had a detachable tail (Figure 81).

Split-eared rabbits (one of which is shown in Plate 17, left), were produced to hold table setting name cards; these invariably turn up singly at antiques and collectors' fairs, but the boxed set illustrated in Plate 16 gives an idea of how they were originally marketed.

Figure 81

Rabbits were also made with an extended base in which there were holes; these were for the purpose of attaching a pin cushion, powder puff, and so on, to it. Plate 17, centre, illustrates one with real rabbit fur attached, which was probably presented upon the birth of a child.

It would be interesting to know the origins of a stoneware bowl (flesh-pink on the inside and white with pink spots on the outside), to which are attached – on opposite sides of the rim – two small pink rabbits which appear to have been made at Denby. On the base is the underglazed mark 'LANGHAM WARE', under which is 'L.M. 4963'.

Rabbit colours are also the subject of much conjecture. It is possible that many colours were purely experimental such as orange, maroon, speckled green/brown, pea green, celadon green and semi-matt blue (the base colour for Orient Ware), and also fawn, black and white – these colours were invariably used for the split-eared and pin-cushion rabbits. Colour variations do also exist within the main colour ranges, for example, the mahogany brown exists both in dark and light shades, as does the shiny (Epic) green.

Although the sizes (height) of the different Denby rabbits were quoted in *Denby Stonewares*, a popular method of identification amongst collectors is through the size of the base. Hopefully, the diagrams of actual base sizes given in the Appendix, will be useful for all collectors, but in particular for those who still have to find the rare sizes of 00, 2A and 4.

Lambs are now becoming more collectable and, like the rabbits, there is a variety of colours including pale green, celadon green, yellow, shiny blue, cream/white, black and even pink. The sizes and respective heights (in centimetres and inches) of the lambs are as follows:

Size:	1	2	3	4	5	6	7
Height (in cm):	5.5	8	12	16.5	20	24.5	28
Height (in in.):	2.2	3.2	4.8	6.6	8	9.8	11.2

Lambs, like rabbits, have appeared on ashtrays; Figure 82 shows the delightful lamp-base version with two cream lambs. An interesting and unusual rare novelty item is the lamb group which features two lambs on a rock (Figure 83). Figure 84 illustrates yet another variation on a theme – this lamb is 15 cm (6 in.) long, is in a cream glaze, and the contouring on the back of the lamb is a simulation of wool.

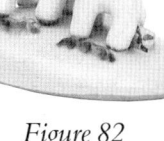

Figure 82

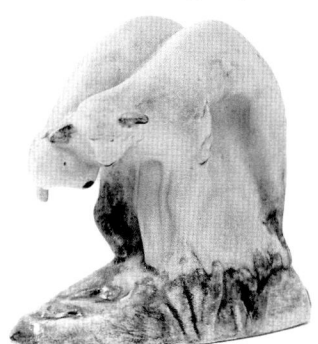

Figure 83

The registered trade name Velray appears on the bases of many of the pieces of Denby pottery which were produced in the 1930s. Items which bear this name include Owl jugs (including one seen in Electric Green glaze!), hot water bottles (including the Gilbert-designed Squirrel in Figure 85), Lovebird bookends and even a blue-glazed toby

Figure 84

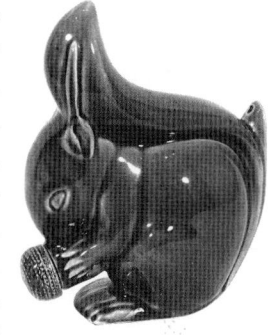

Figure 85

Figure 86

Figure 87

jug (Figure 86). The Lovebird bookends illustrated in Figure 87 are quite unique in that they still have the paper label (which reads 'Beauty's Romance by Velray'), attached to the front of them; the elephant pictured between the bookends also bears the Velray mark. Another paper label, which reads 'PERFUME/ SPECIAL VELRAY/ROSE MARIE', is still attached to the base (Figure 88), and covers a hole through which bath salts (which are still inside!) were dispensed.

Figure 88

Denby Stonewares featured the special range of art pottery, known as Garden Pottery and designed by Donald Gilbert, which had an emphasis on animals and birds. Several of these very attractive and desirable pieces from private collections have been made available to be photographed, including:

- Dolphin bowl on Pedestal (Plate 18).
- Penguin (Plate 19), which stands 42.5 cm (17 in.) high and is holding a fish in its mouth.
- Squirrel on a log (Figure 89), which is 28.75 cm (11.5 in.) high.

Figure 89

In the Denby Stonewares Exhibition at Derby in Spring 1997, one of the most popular display cabinets – with both children and adults – was the one which featured a plethora of animal novelties and ashtrays. Some of the most fascinating items featured were:

Figure 90

- Panda (Figure 90).

PLATE 21.
Boatman ashtray

PLATE 22.
Large vase by Alice Teichner

PLATE 23.
Fruit bowl in Tibet glaze

PLATE 24.
Jug by Glyn Colledge

Figure 91

Figure 92

Figure 93

Figure 94

Figure 95

Figure 96

- Hen and Chicks (Figure 91).
- Kitten and Ball of Wool ashtray (Figure 92, left), and Foxhounds ashtray (Figure 92, right).
- Lion cub (Figure 93).
- Zebra (Figure 94, left), and Donkey (Figure 94, right).
- Dachshunds (Figure 95).
- Pair of Elephants (Figure 96).
- Swan ashtray (Figure 97).
- Donkey and Cart (Figure 98).
- Terrier ashtray (Figure 99).

Figure 97

Figure 98

Figure 99

41

Figure 100

Figure 101

Figure 102

Figure 103

Figure 104

Figure 105

- Squirrel marmalade jar (Figure 100).
- Wartime Byngos (Figure 101).
- Lovebird (Figure 102).
- Sea lion (Plate 20).
- Dundee (fish) bookend (Figure 103).
- Toadstool spill can (Figure 104).
- Birds marmalade jar (Figure 105, left).
- Buttons ashtray (Figure 105, right).
- Duck Set on base (Figure 106, left), Geese wall plaque (Figure 106, centre), and Strident (Figure 106, right).
- Boatman ashtray (Plate 21).

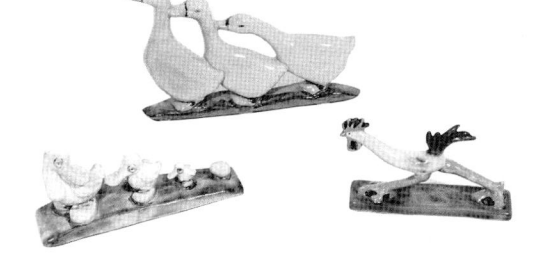

Figure 106

4
Towards World War II and Beyond

THE avant-garde designs of the Austrian-born Alice Teichner certainly made a lasting impression upon the glazes and shapes of pottery produced at Denby Pottery from 1936 onwards. Several of the novelties already illustrated were designed by her, including the Toadstool spill can, the Dundee bookend, the wartime Byngos and the Terrier ashtray.

As already described in *Denby Stonewares*, Alice Teichner's style of work is often heavily potted with thick rims and handles, and applied loops and ribs. The following artefacts illustrate her remarkable and distinctive talents:

- Small vase with applied fruit to the rim (Figure 107).
- Two-handled vase (Figure 108).
- Large vase (Plate 22), around 35 cm (14 in.) high, with applied fruit/leaves to the rim.

(All three of these pieces are in the outstanding old gold glaze.)

- Lamp base (Figure 109), with multi-coloured floral decoration.

Figure 107

Figure 108

In the two years before World War II, Denby launched many new ranges of pottery which relied mainly on shape for their appeal; generally, there was a return to plainer non-art-pottery glazes. Two such exceptions are the Fruit bowl in the Tibet glaze (circa 1940–1) (Plate 23), and the bowl featured in Figure 110 which has a crackle glaze in the centre. Research into the different designs and glazes at this sparsely documented time of Denby's history is currently taking place.

Figure 109

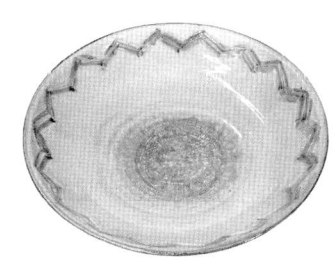

Figure 110

43

Figure 111

Figure 112

Figure 113

A series of bulb bowls was introduced in 1938 and included in this series were:

- Owl bowl (Figure 111), based on the Owl vase by Donald Gilbert which is illustrated earlier in Plate 12, and produced at the beginning of the decade. The piece illustrated in Figure 111 is in a Mottled Blue glaze
- Oval bowl (Figure 112), featuring a semi-relief fawn and stylised trees.
- Flying Bird bowl (Figure 113), in a satin blue glaze with applied birds in semi-relief.

Some of these pre-war ranges are now beginning to find favour with collectors and they include:

- Greenstone Ware which has a rough-textured finish; Figure 114 shows a Clumber vase, which is 25 cm (10 in.) high, and Figure 115 shows a Crich Jug, which is 38 cm (15.2 in.) high.
- Waverley Ware was quite an extensive series of shapes in single-coloured glazes which included cream, green, ivory, chalk blue, oyster and lime green. The deer-head handled vase in Figure 116 is 39 cm (15.6 in.) high, and is in a dusky pink glaze.
- Old Ivory design had a series of horizontal ridges with a spattered yellow glaze (Figure 117).
- Danesby Ware Cottage glaze, first produced around

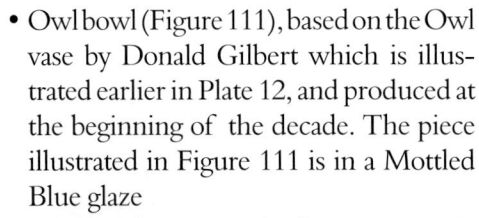

Figure 114

Figure 115

Figure 116

Figure 117

1940–1, has a matt red exterior with applied coloured flowers with a deep cream interior glaze (Figure 118).

- Figure 119 illustrates decorative ware having a semi-matt glaze in pastel-coloured bands. This design was introduced around 1939.
- Figure 120 shows a group of three pieces in a post-war range which is thought to have been called Festival; the green glaze is criss-crossed with a slightly raised basket effect, and brightly-coloured fruit bunches are applied as decoration.
- Gayborder (Figure 121) appeared around 1948, based on shapes which were in the pre-war catalogues; the glaze colour is oyster with the addition of hand-applied floral decoration.
- Tally-Ho, which was featured in *Denby Stonewares*, was produced mainly for the American market from 1945-7. Although mugs, jugs and goblets are quite common, the three-piece teaset (Figure 122) is something of a rarity.

Figure 118

Figure 119

Figure 120

Figure 121

Figure 122

In the post-war period, the artistic skills of Glyn Colledge developed rapidly in both decorative and domestic pottery production. We have chosen to feature a few select examples of his work and output, some of which appeared in the Denby Stonewares Exhibition:

- Lamp base (Figure 123), 27 cm (10.8 in.) high; the semi-matt orange-yellow is embellished with more highly-glazed 'jewels'.
- Ginger jar (Figure 124), with hand-painted scene of a room interior.
- Two-handled sweet dish (Figure 125), with hand-painted horse scene.
- Jug (Plate 24), with hand-painted floral decoration, dating from the late 1940s.
- Two mugs (Figure 126), produced for the Derby Rowing Club, the left-hand mug featuring a tube-lined plaque of oarsmen.
- Cheviot vase (Figure 127), 41 cm (16.4 in.) high, in black with etched decoration.
- Cheviot bowl (Figure 128), in a sky blue glaze with a black, abstract design on it.
- Glynbourne lamp base (Figure 129); these are uncommon, and were not produced in large quantities.

Figure 123

Figure 124

Figure 125

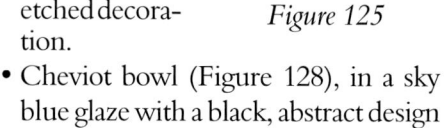

Figure 126

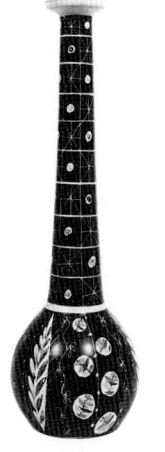

Figure 127

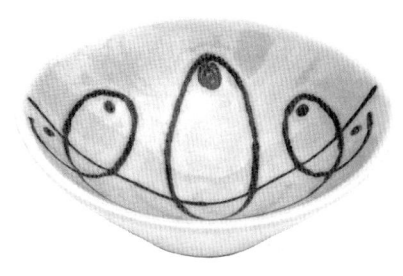

Figure 128

Figure 129

Figure 130 *Figure 131*

Finally, three more modern oddities:

- Teaset (Figure 130); this four-piece teaset is quite unusual in that it has a gold lustre glaze and, from the scroll base mark and design shape, was most probably made in the mid-1950s.
- Group of shoes, some with gold decoration (Figure 131), produced in the Hill-Ouston giftware range in the mid-1950s.
- Pumpkin vase (Figure 132), in brown/green glaze, also belonging to the Hill-Ouston giftware range.

Figure 132

Appendix. Actual Base Sizes of Denby Rabbits

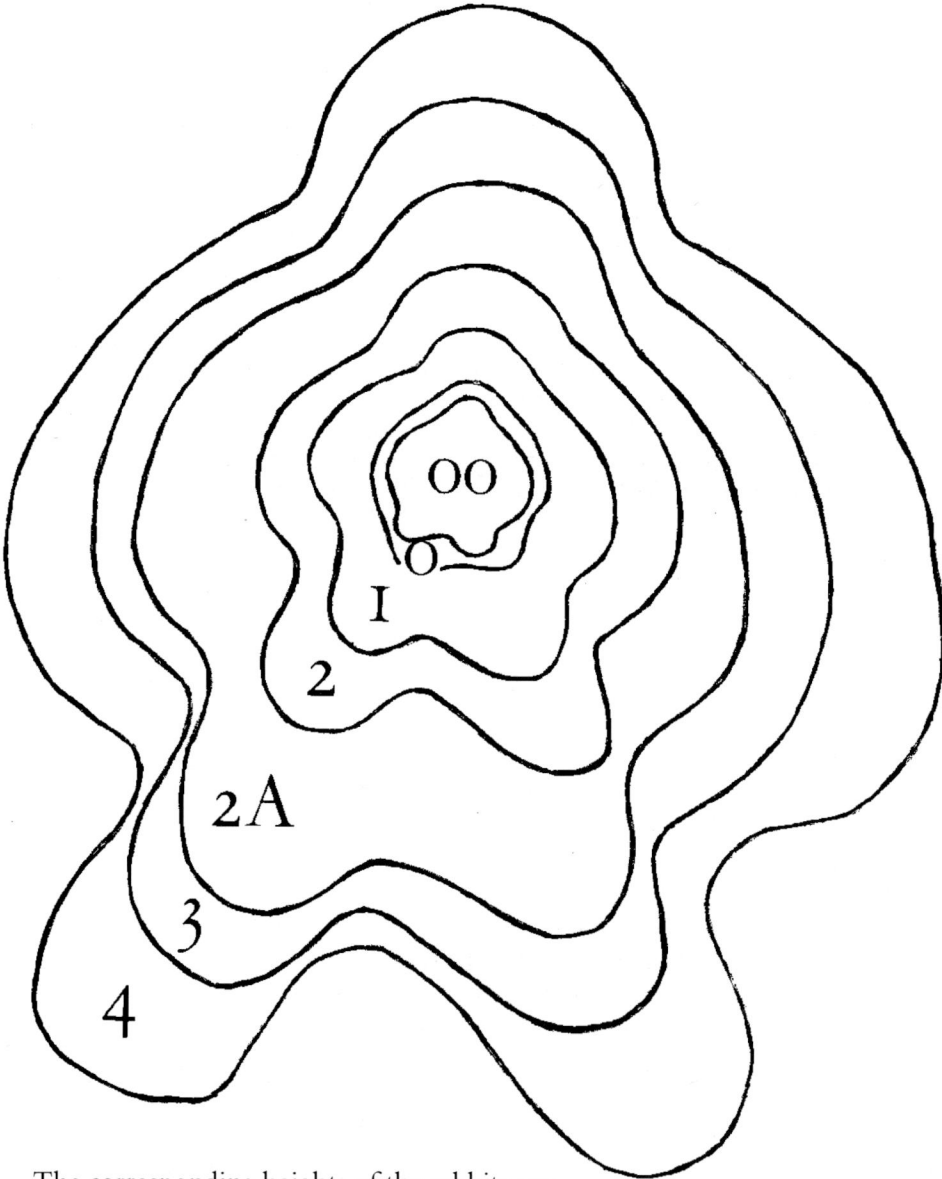

The corresponding heights of the rabbits are:

Size:	00	0	1	2	2A	3	4
Height (in cm):	3.5	4.5	8.5	12.25	16.25	20.25	26.25
Height (in in.):	1.4	1.8	3.4	4.9	6.5	8.1	10.5